There a

In Jesus; Only Oportunities
To "Shine". (Count It All Joy)
"We" Don't Owe No
One A ~~Life~~ Any Thing;
No One Owes Us
Any Thing; But
To Love Others
    Every One We
Must Love Exspecially
The One ⬤ Who
    Offends Us.

Praise for Carolyn L. Jennings . . .

Carolyn is pure love—she has a beautiful prayer consciousness as well as an expansive Prosperity consciousness that reflects itself in this wonderful book. For many years I have seen her demonstrate these prosperity principles in her life.

Reverend Robert J. Brumet

- - - - -

Reverend Carolyn Jennings is a powerful creator. Through many decades with her as my spiritual teacher, prayer counselor, and friend, I have seen Carolyn model a way of living that manifests every needed resource, right on time and in its fullness. Carolyn lives lavishly within modest means. She is not mesmerized by materiality. She does not require many belongings. Instead, Carolyn harnesses the source of her plenty consciousness to bring into view whatever she desires in order to fulfill her daily needs as well as her life's purpose. Carolyn lives in faithful expectancy of good, for which I feel grateful and inspired.

Reverend Linda Martella-Whitsett

- - - - -

I first met Carolyn when we both were prayer associates at Silent Unity. Her prayer consciousness, depth of faith and understanding of the power of prayer, led me to ask her to be my prayer partner. The relationship has been a gift to me in my ministry. She's the "real deal."

Reverend Sandra McKinney

On July 4, 2016, Carolyn and I will have known each other for 40 years. Most of that time we've lived hundreds of miles apart, but that never changed our always being there for each other. Carolyn's capacity to focus on the spiritual is fantastic. It is simply who she is. How fortunate I've been to have her as a spiritual grounding force in my life. She is the one who taught me that it's okay to say, "I am *Financial* Prosperity." That may seem like a little thing, but it was an epiphany for me. Imagine something financial being a part of my spiritual life! And so it is.

MariLyn K. Richardson

- - - - -

Carolyn shares how faith becomes fact in her everyday life - experiences of a beautiful soul.

Reverend Jane Waddington

- - - - -

One of the definitions of prosperity is the condition of being successful or thriving. In the 30-plus years I have known the Reverend Carolyn Jennings, she has clearly demonstrated her understanding of that definition. She has an abiding faith in that which we call Principle. She knows her Source. Regardless of outer circumstances (which have sometimes looked pretty bleak to my human perspective), she has had an inner knowing that everything will work out for the best. And because she has that faith, everything does, indeed, work out. I can't imagine a better author of a book on prosperity than Rev. Jennings.

Reverend Sandy McWilliams

I have learned extensively about truly prosperous living from Carolyn by observing how she lives her life. She has demonstrated, by example, how to apply the Unity teachings of the Fillmores, Catherine Ponder, tithing, seed money and more. Even through numerous stressful times in her life over the last 15 years, I have seen her prosper anyway - manifesting many times over what she needed and wanted - health, peace, joy of living, self-care, finances, perfect places to live, friends, to name a few.

As a result of our friendship and her mentoring,, my beliefs about prosperity have changed, broadened and been cemented irreversibly in my consciousness. Carolyn "walks the talk" and, without a doubt, practices what she preaches/teaches.

TeresaRose Keller

- - - - -

Reverend Carolyn Jennings writes from a place of deep spiritual knowledge and practical experience in her book. Her readers will find inspiration as well as helpful tools to use in their own prosperity breakthroughs.

Reverend Edie Skalitzky

- - - - -

I can say with integrity that Carolyn Jennings has always been a person who lives her Truth simply and clearly. She demonstrates a consciousness of service to others with no thought of self-aggrandizement.

Reverend Tom Thorpe

Prosper Anyway ...

Beyond Limitations of
Low Income or World Economy

Rev. Carolyn L. Jennings

For comments:
> SUBJECTLINE - Prosper Anyway to:
> carolynljennings@gmail.com.

FIRST U.S. EDITION

COVER DESIGN & EDITING by:
> Sharon Kay, M.A., L.U.T.

ISBN-10: 1511632674
ISBN-13: 978-1511632676

DEDICATION

Dedicated to Reverend Donald R. Jennings,
beloved husband of 47 years, father, friend,
teacher, colleague, and Unity Minister.

I also dedicate *Prosper Anyway* to the other three
great loves in my life: my son, D. Jeffrey Jennings;
daughter, Rev. Kimberly A. J. Giacometti; and
granddaughter, Emily Jennings Giacometti;
and to all people, that you may prosper beyond
your wildest dreams.

~ ~ ~ ~ ~

ACKNOWLEDGEMENTS

I am grateful for each friend and family member who gave me encouragement and support for writing *Prosper Anyway*. This includes the following:

Support
Edie Skalitzky
Jane Waddington
Jennifer Sacks
Jim Gaither
Kimberly A. J. Giacometti
Linda Martella-Whitsett
Matthew Long
MariLyn K Richardson
Marygrace Sorenson
Nola Yergen
Robert Brumet
Sandy McWilliams
Tom Shepherd
Tom Thorpe
William Smith

An important concept in *Prosper Anyway* is "speaking the word." While in my process of writing the following happened:

A new neighbor-friend and I were visiting when I shared that I was in t he process of writing *Prosper Anyway* and ready to find an editor. I was totally amazed when I heard Sharon Kay say that she had some experience in writing/editing and would be happy to work with me on an informal basis. I knew nothing of her background, knowledge and experience – which I soon found to be extensive.

As soon as "the word" of this desire was spoken, the perfect answer came immediately! Over the past couple of years Sharon has worked with me *many* hours, giving of her time, experience and expertise with great patience.

Sharon gave this gift of service free of charge, a very huge gift!

This project has taken much more time than I, and possibly Sharon, had first imagined. Thank you and bless you, Sharon, for this unimaginable gift and most of all for our growing friendship!

(NOTE FROM SHARON: Though cash may not have changed hands, getting to know Carolyn and numerous of her friends has been an invaluable experience for me and one which I will always treasure.)

PREFACE

Stories shared in *Prosper Anyway* span over forty years of my life. They still delight and amaze me!

Most of the experiences shared in these stories took place before I became an ordained Unity minister and were thanks to the teachings of Unity.

The "facts" showed many to appear impossible … yet they happened. Each experience came first from intuiting "how-to" steps for activating Universal Prosperity Principles.

This included:
- dream homes
- businesses
- Hawaiian vacations
- living in permanent prosperity

These experiences proved to me that, whatever our present circumstance, we can *Prosper Anyway, Beyond Limitations of Low Income and World Economy!*

My intention for writing this book is to inspire you to find your own steps to activate Prosperity Principles and live in ways that best serve you and your world.

Chapter 10 is dedicated to <u>ministers and anyone involved with ministry finances.</u> Specifics are given on how my husband Reverend Don Jennings and I helped the ministries we served to *Prosper Anyway*.

(NO QUICK FIX S)

This is not meant to be a quick fix. These are ideas and practices to support and encourage you in a daily journey of practicing these Spiritual Prosperity Principles. *TIME & EFFORT MUST ~~BE APPLIED~~*

It is worth the time and effort it took to write *Prosper Anyway* if even one person benefits—and I hope it is you. You are worth it! *Enliven / Enlighten*

Growing in awareness and understanding continues to be a rewarding, enlivening practice in my life and a great joy for which I am grateful!

I give thanks that spiritual understanding, with practice, continues to blossom and enliven us.

As you feel inspired, you are invited to tell at least one other person about this book, and to write to me about your experiences.

... BE APPLIED

PATIENTLY CONFORMING

NEW WAYS OF ACTION

Growing In Awareness and understanding Continues To Be Rewarded

Enlivening Practices

Miracles or Spiritual Principles?

Scientific use of Spiritual Principles is more effective than hoping for miracles and can result in Permanent Prosperity. These Prosperity Principles, sometimes called Universal Laws, work only when we work them … with understanding and commitment.

This is reaffirmed repeatedly by Charles Fillmore, cofounder of the Unity movement, who states in *Dynamics for Living*, "Happenings that seem miraculous are controlled by laws that we have not yet learned and result from causes we have not been able to understand." (Page 193)

Cofounder of Unity, Myrtle Fillmore, is quoted in Harold Whaley's book *Whatsoever Things Are True* as saying, "Those who are prosperous and successful are the people who have a rich consciousness…the ones who have developed their innate abilities and used the success-producing ideas that have come to them." (Page 40)

Unity minister, Eric Butterworth, a great influence on the Unity movement, in his book *Spiritual Economics,* says, "Any person who is experiencing lack is, in some way, living in opposition to the universal flow." (Page 7)

Work with universal flow instead of against it.

Dear friend, it does seem like magic when one commits to practicing Spiritual Principles.

Commitment

"...until one is committed there is hesitancy, the chance to draw back, always ineffectiveness concerning all acts of initiative and creativity. There is one elementary truth, the ignorance of which kills countless ideas and splendid plans: the moment one definitely commits oneself, then providence moves too.

"All sorts of things occur to help one that would never otherwise have occurred. A whole stream of events issues from the decision, raising in one's favor all manner of unforeseen incidents, meetings and material assistance which no one could have dreamt possible."

W.H. Murray

"Whatever you can do or dream you can...begin it. Boldness has Genius, Power and Magic in it."

Goethe

Begin Your Journey in the Quiet

Know you are born blessed and worthy, a spiritual
   being, as is every person. Therefore, you are
   worthy of your highest soul desires.

Ask yourself *what* it is you most deeply want?
   More importantly *how* do you truly want to live?

Listen for your truest answers, then commit.
   Commit to yourself for sacred moments of time to
   gain a deepening awareness of yourself, plus
   absorb Truth Principles into your mind-heart.

Table of Contents
(Be aware I've intertwined Chapters 1, 2, and 3)

Table of Contents – Cont.

Chapter 1

Alaskan Dream Home...Facts Showed It Impossible Yet Here We Were, My 21-Day Process

Our small Alaskan condominium seemed to be shrinking with the energy of our two teenagers, Kim and Jeff. After living in this space for one year we noticed ourselves experiencing higher stress.

However, there was no money for a larger home -- none at all was apparent! This was gently but firmly stated, repeatedly, by my loving husband, Reverend Don Jennings.

In 1976 we had moved from Port Angeles, Washington, to Anchorage, Alaska, to serve in the first Unity Church there. It became Unity of Anchorage.

The idea of having a Unity church home began with two families, the Richards and Talbots, dedicated to having this Unity experience for Alaskans.

They began by meeting in one another's homes, taking turns giving the Sunday service, and including their children. This gathering soon grew until the number of those attending outgrew their homes.

At that time they rented space on Sunday evenings in the Congregational Church, thanks to the hospitality of Reverend Don Lindsay, and his wife Peggy.

After this year, these dedicated Unity students brought ministers up from the Pacific Northwest to give Sunday services and workshops. They did this every weekend for one year and paid airfare, hotel and meals. Don was one of those ministers.

A few months afterward, while guest speaking for them, Don took me out to lunch and told me the Anchorage congregation was interested in hiring him to be their minister. They wanted us both to come for a week of interviews, to get acquainted and see the area. He broke it to me slowly since he knew I was not interested in moving again. We had moved from Missouri to Washington only two years before, and extensively the years before, due to Don's work in the computer industry; then to school at Unity Village.

Upon hearing this, I said, "Oh no," then came excitement—knowing it was right—and shared a dream I'd had a few weeks earlier: I was in Alaska, outdoors in deep snow, picking up stacks of hundred dollar bills that were barely below the snow's surface, everywhere. Men standing around just watching were getting mad. I asked why they were mad when the money (representing Substance) was there for everyone.

We said yes to the invitation. In addition to these exciting meetings, we were driven around to experience that area of Alaska. At the end of the week, all concluded that this was a Divine Appointment and we said, "Yes!"

Our first Alaskan home was a lovely two-story rental in Turnagain. The first level was our Unity offices and class room; the second level our home. Sunday evenings we continued meeting in the First Congregational Church.

After living in this home one year, the landlord decided to move into it, giving us only a few months notice.

We thought we would enjoy living in a condominium in the same area, and our Unity office and meeting space had recently moved downtown.

Following Inner Guidance and other Prosperity Principles taught in Unity, we were able to move into a newly built three-bedroom condominium. First, it was necessary to come up with $16,000. It was amazing how it all came together.

Kim and Jeff were now young teens and, with four high energy people, after one year, we were noticing the high stress of living in this smaller space. I wanted a larger home!

The cost of living in Anchorage was very high, especially housing. Still my desire to have a larger home kept gnawing at me. It did not go away, so I continued contemplating and meditating on my desire, and ideas began to percolate!

The following two stories played a significant role in this manifestation which continues on page 13.

Opportunity to Write Your Aha's: Chapter 1

A Major Move: Unity Village, Missouri to Port Angeles, Washington...Visualization

Spring 1974, Don was about to graduate from Unity's ministerial school at Unity Village, Missouri. Our desire was to begin serving in a ministry by September in time for Kim and Jeff to start school.

Our family had a passion to move to Port Angeles, Washington, to be near family, and return to beautiful Puget Sound and our beloved home state. Eagerness to move there was amplified since Don's folks and sister Patty recently moved to this city and the Unity Church no longer had a minister.

However, this congregation had been through a difficult time. So, during the year Don was to graduate and be ordained, it did not look possible that they would be able to pay a full-time minister, especially one supporting a family by the time we would be ready.

Meantime, Reverend Leona McMillan, a lovely woman and Unity minister, had begun working with the Port Angeles Unity congregation as Interim Minister for healing and to build their spiritual consciousness. Then we heard they were very interested in us!

The congregation and Board of Trustees began joining us in prayer as we all held in mind and heart this ministry flourishing, with the ability to hire Don, full-time by the end of August.

To empower our personal prayer consciousness, Don and I created a Treasure Map on one whole wall in our bedroom, out of sight where others would not see it, to hold the power for our intention and visualize this desire into being.

On the Treasure Map we included:

- Jesus, representing the True Source of our Instant, Constant and Abundant Supply

- seagulls to bring forth the feeling of living in the Pacific Northwest

- Unity in The Olympics, the name of this Unity Church

- pictures representing aspects of the type of home we desired

- words of gratitude for this *or something better* for the Highest Good of all concerned!

Each time we heard reports from others that this Unity Center was still not financially able to hire a full-time minister, we held to our knowing of Truth Principles, reviewed our Treasure Map, and knew that if this was ours to do, with Spirit there would be a way.

At the eleventh hour, as Don completed graduation and ordination, he was hired. We were thrilled! In August 1972, our family moved from Lee's Summit, Missouri, to Port Angeles, Washington.

This was years before "Field of Dreams," the movie sharing the idea, "If you build it they will come."

The congregation, Don and I, with Reverend Leona McMillan, had built the consciousness which made it possible for them to hire Don.

Even though Don's paycheck was minimal, and I was volunteering my services, we felt prosperous living in this exquisitely beautiful area with snowcapped Olympic Mountains, lush Evergreen forests, pristine lakes, and the saltwater bays of Puget Sound.

It also helped that Don's folks, my beloved in-laws Lucille and Walt Jensen, now owned a "mom and pop" cafe that served breakfasts and lunches near the water front in Port Angeles.

They served delicious home cooked meals, plus mom's scrumptious pies, making it a popular place. In addition to many dinners in their home, our family was generously gifted with many meals in their restaurant. In addition, congregants shared an abundance of fresh vegetables from their gardens, plus fish and seafood.

At times when our cupboards were nearly bare, the intuitive Joyce Paulson, a congregant who became a dear friend, would show up in the evening on our doorstep surprising us with bags of groceries! Then this dear soul stayed and gave us soothing, healing, treatments!

Looking at our situation from the outside it might have looked like we were living in poverty, yet we were abundantly supplied and very happy doing the work we most loved!

A paycheck is only a part of one's opulence. Abundance can come in infinite ways!

Opportunity to Write Your Aha's: Chapter 2

Chapter 3

The Piano...Creating a Spiritual Vacuum

While living in Port Angeles, Kim and Jeff expressed a desire for piano lessons. You might guess there was no money to buy a piano.

Nature abhors a vacuum, a Spiritual Principle taught in Unity, includes making a physical space for something deeply desired, envisioning it, and trusting -- letting go of doubt about how it could unfold.

One morning, inspired, I moved furniture out of an area in the living room across from the front door, moved a hanging lamp higher, then pictured a piano filling that space. I had no clue how it could possibly happen or how many weeks it would take, then left on errands.

Upon returning home a few hours later, I opened our front door, stopped and stared... absolutely astounded! There, in that exact same space, sat a piano...the top fitting exactly underneath the hanging lamp where it had been raised. It was an upright piano. I could hardly believe my eyes. The spiritual demonstration had been immediate.

My husband, Don, was the only one who knew about the space created that morning. My guess at first, and perhaps yours, was he had arranged it. No, he had not!

That same morning a couple in the congregation made an unscheduled visit to the Unity Church office to discuss a problem with Don. Planning to get married, both had households of furniture including two pianos.

Hearing about the space created that morning they delivered a piano, at no cost.

To this day Kim and Jeff fondly remember the piano experience and the power of the Spiritual Principle of "creating a vacuum."

A Silent Unity booklet entitled "Simple Living, When Less is More," says that "As you make space, stand in faith and trust certain that something positive will come into your life to replace what you have released..."

Opportunity to Write Your Aha's: Chapter 3

_____
_____
_____
_____
_____
_____
_____
_____
_____
_____
_____
_____
_____
_____
_____
_____
_____
_____
_____
_____
_____
_____
_____
_____
_____
_____
_____
_____
_____
_____
_____

Remembering the seemingly impossible manifestation of our piano, plus understanding there is no small or large with Spiritual Principle, I was charged with enthusiasm. I made the decision to go for all I ever wanted in a house, my dream home.

A result of meditation and opening to possibility thinking, inner guidance came that included listing all that I ever wanted in a home.

Understanding it takes 21 days to build a new habit, I decided to work that many days for a heightened prosperity consciousness, making my list just before bedtime, a potent time for spiritual work.

At the top of my first page, plus each subsequent page, I wrote these reminders to keep my focus on Spiritual Principle:

- Source (Spiritual Source) is Unlimited!

- I Am / We Are Worthy!

- Desire comes through Source; therefore, a deeply felt desire also comes with the way to experience it.

According to Eric Butterworth, in his book *Spiritual Economics*, "Before you formulate a desire in mind, it is God in you desiring . . . Spirit in you prompting you in that direction." (Page 69)

Spiritual Substance, from which all manifests, is never depleted.

Reading repeatedly, and visualizing the following, from Charles Fillmore's *Dynamics for Living* was a major key for me:

"Be still and turn within to the great Source. See with the eye of faith that the whole world is filled with substance. See it falling all about you as snowflakes of gold and silver. In laying hold of substance in the mind and bringing it into manifestation [our work] is to express substance ideas in material form. Identify yourself with substance until you make it yours.

"Actually, you are unified with the one living substance, which is God [Source], your all-sufficiency. From this substance you were created, in it you live and move and have your being. By it you are fed and prospered.

"Spiritual substance is steadfast, immoveable, enduring. It does not fluctuate. It does not decrease.

"As you lay hold of substance with your mind, make it permanent and enduring. Realize your oneness with it. Then you will soon begin to rejoice in the ever-present bounty of God." (Page 192)

The following, by Paul Hasselbeck in *Heart-Centered Metaphysics*, further defines Divine Substance:

"Substance is 'Divine Energy', the Invisible Matrix from Which all possible forms of supply develop. The Divine Idea of Substance is everywhere present in Its entirety. Substance is not matter, but It makes matter possible."

Hasselbeck goes on to say, "True Prosperity is about having the consciousness of Divine Substance. It can never be depleted and responds according to our Faith and the demands we make on It." (Page 367)

I recommend reading further in Hasselbeck's chapter on this topic.

Here are a few of my reminders.

- Facts are changeable; Spiritual Principle is unchangeable, eternal.

- I am open and receptive to my (sacred desire) or something better!

  (The Universe has much more good for us than we can fully conceive!)

- Gratitude

  (Feeling gratitude beforehand and living in the energy of gratitude is powerful.)

While writing my desires, whenever listing something that felt outrageous to expect, I stopped writing and refocused on those reminders of Spiritual Principle written at the top of each page until I regained what felt like my "Yes" consciousness.

The final list of desires for my dream house consisted of six handwritten pages, which included such things as a sauna and an intercom.

One day our realtor showed us a four bedroom house that included many of the things on my list. It was even in Kim and Jeff's same school district, important since we'd already moved several times in their young lives.

However, I felt disappointment in the number of things on my list that it did not have. I was so eager for a larger home that I almost settled, tempted to accept less.

Fear came up with my decision not to accept this house, wondering if I might be expecting too much, that we might not find something this good again, let alone something even better.

Through more inner work I returned to my resolve and positive thinking with faith and courage, refocusing on possibility thinking.

In this same time frame, I led a Master Mind prayer group at Unity of Anchorage.

A Master Mind group consists of two to six people who meet each week in a place of business, home or ministry. This supportive experience is powerful for connecting for success.

This process uses Affirmative Prayer and is based on the scripture found in Matthew 13:20, "Where two or more of you are gathered in my name there I am in the midst of you."

As we grow in spiritual understanding we discern wording that more clearly gives our spiritual perspective; therefore, I would now change words such as "God" and "Master Mind" to "Source" or "Spirit within."

If you choose to use the Master Mind idea, I encourage you to discern and use the most meaningful wording to members of the group, keeping in mind each Principle.

The Master Mind version we used was a revision of Reverend Jack Boland's work. The following includes adjustments made for our group.

Master Mind Process

Each time we met we began in an energy/attitude of gratitude by sharing good news of the previous week.

Next we read aloud together steps 1-4.

1. Surrendering - Improving my life does not come from relying on the outer world. It comes from knowing my oneness with God, the Master Mind [Spirit] within me.

2. Knowing - I know that the Intelligence and Creative Power of the Universe is working in and through me now and always, and I agree to work with it.

3. Deciding - I decide to allow the activity of God in me to completely take charge of my life and to change me at depth. I align my will with the will of God which is always for my highest and best.

4. Releasing - I release any fear and doubt. I accept the forgiving Love of the Master Mind; therefore, I forgive all others and I am forgiven.

5. Asking (each person takes a turn sharing) - Master Mind I ask, I seek, I knock. I am open and receptive to your guidance. I follow through that which I am guided to do. I know that you are at work in me and through me for this intention _____. (Person names their desired intention.)

Everyone then reads aloud, together, affirming for that person:

> "I know the Master Mind has heard you and you will experience guidance and fulfillment for this or something even better."

6. Gratefully Receiving (person speaking who gave intention) says:

> "I affirm my complete trust in Spirit, grateful for my guidance each step of the way. I am grateful!"

Steps 5-6 were repeated with each person present.

7. Dedication and Covenant (read aloud together):

> "I now have a covenant with my inner Master Mind. I agree to listen and obey, open to experiencing seeming miracles in my life now. I know that the Master Mind is providing me with the time and an abundance of all necessary for my intention or something even better."

During the week, in our personal prayer times, we held one another's intentions.

While working this process, I frequently referred back to the Serenity Prayer and the Power of An Attitude which follow:

Serenity Prayer

God, grant me the serenity to accept the things I cannot change, courage to change the things I can, and wisdom to know the difference. (Reinhold Niebuhr, c1937)

Power of an Attitude
Author unknown

A positive, expectant attitude of good puts me in the right place at the right time.
I create new beginnings with a new attitude.

Often our answer is right in front of us. We only must open to that answer.

George C., Master Mind participant, upon hearing my prayer intention, said he was selling his home and that it was exactly what I was describing. He was eager for us to see it.

Since it was not in Kim and Jeff's school district, I told him I was not interested. Over time George persisted, urging that we at least look at it.

Information about George's house came on the heels of saying no to the earlier house and, through meditation, releasing fear over that decision. Finally I said we would at least look at his home.

Walking up to the front door, we immediately fell in love with it! The front door was a gorgeous red with beautiful massive white rock wall on either side.

That was just the beginning!

The financial details are a blur in my mind now; probably then, too, as they weren't my job.

George had recently become single, wanted a smaller home and, of all things, had suggested trading our condominium for his house. This is what happened along with a bit of financial negotiation!

The details were worked out by my husband, Don, and congregants, banker Bob R. and realtor Grace S.; plus, prayer support by our Master Mind group.

Facts showed it impossible; yet here we were!

We moved into our spacious, beautiful, two level home. It had every single thing on my six page list and more, except one important thing! It included my dreamed of sauna, intercom, and not one but two beautiful stone fireplaces! George even gifted us his pool table, yard equipment and outdoor furniture.

You might be wondering which thing on my list did not happen. This house was not in Kim and Jeff's same school district! This I'd thought would be vital. We did not want them to have to change schools again. This had happened enough in their young lives.

Then an idea came. We realized Unity of Anchorage where Don and I served and spent most of our time was in their same school district. We decided to use this as our home base which worked well for our family. The idea of "This or something better" kept me open to this amazing answer.

It makes a difference to stay open to more than that which we first can conceive.

This beautiful home was a perfect size for our family during our kids' teen years, even accommodating 150 of their West High School Thespian friends for after play parties.

By the way these parties happened late Saturday nights, after the current play ended, and went into the wee morning hours. When we were first asked if the party could be at our home I said I couldn't possibly stay up that late, then leave early the next morning to work at church. However, Don said "Yes"—and he loved it! Then the next morning he was at Unity giving the Sunday service. I don't know how he was able to manage it! However, he was just that kinda dad and devoted minister!

Living here had looked financially impossible. (It may be hard for you to believe.) Remembering it still amazes me!

It proved to me once again that working with Universal Principle, we are unlimited! We are so much more than outer, apparently limiting, "facts".

Years later we sold our home, allowing us to buy a beautiful, efficient 34' motor home for traveling the "lower 48" for a one year sabbatical. Kim and Jeff had graduated from high school and each had their own plans.

Opportunity to Write Your Aha's: Chapter 1 Continued

Chapter 4

Hawaii Anyway…
Following the Still Small Voice

While living in Alaska, a desire emerged that began in my childhood, to see Hawaii.

This desire was spurred on seeing the amazing number of people living in Anchorage, even entire families with lots of children, vacationing in Hawaii.

One day Don and I bought tickets to fly to Hawaii. I was thrilled! Soon after, Don told me he could not go after all. Details for the Unity of Anchorage project to bring Norman Vincent Peale, with his wife Ruth, to speak in Anchorage and Juneau were taking more time than expected.

The disappointment I felt was profound! Crestfallen, I knew it isn't helpful or healthy to hold onto feelings of upset or attachments.

During meditations the next few days, I made the intention to let go of the idea of traveling to Hawaii, and the disappointment. This brought a deep sense of peace.

Then, the morning I planned to return our plane tickets to the travel agency, I received an unexpected call from a woman in the congregation. She heard about the change in our Hawaii plans and told me not to cancel my plane ticket. She had a plane ticket for Hawaii and we could go together! Not only that, she had a place for us to stay...free! It was hard to believe and I was thrilled! I kept my ticket, grateful to have done the releasing work that allowed for this great answer.

She also told me there was room for one more to stay. I invited a friend, Twilah B., a nurse who was close to burn-out, who told me this was an answer to prayer. She made her plane reservation.

The friend who 'had the place for us to stay' called one day saying she couldn't go after all. I was beside myself with concern for Twilah who so needed this respite vacation. I did not want to cancel on her, had no clue where we could stay, and we had our airline tickets!

This same year a new congregant began attending Unity of Anchorage. She knew of my taking appointments in downtown Anchorage for Sacred Foot Reflexology. She was a close friend of Reflexologist and author, Mildred Carter, and told me Mildred had recently moved to the island of Hawaii.

Then, as I continued opening for an answer, one day in meditation I heard within me very specific words (an unusual happening for me). It seemed to be an answer. However, I did not want to follow the guidance and ignored it. The next day in meditation I heard those same exact words.

"Call Mildred Carter. Tell her you and a friend are coming to Hawaii, don't have a place yet to stay, but that you would love to take some of her reflexology classes. She will invite you to stay in her home."

We had never even met! She was author of *Helping Yourself with Foot Reflexology* which I was using for my own practice.

Mildred had no idea who I was, but since the instructions came twice I picked up my courage and phoned using those exact words without a hint in tone of concern for where we would stay. Mildred spoke the exact words inviting us to stay with her.

Next, my friend, Twyla B., had to make a schedule adjustment with her travel plans. She was coming later than the time scheduled with Mildred Carter and now there was a need to find an additional place to stay. This felt like another huge challenge.

In the meantime, one Sunday Don left earlier for church than I did. Friends in our congregation, June and Paul Robison, picked me up to go to the service. A friend of theirs was sitting in the front seat and introduced herself.

Hearing that her last name was the same as my maiden name, I asked her how it was spelled. Rather than "Teal", as is often the case, she said "Teel"—the same as mine. Astonished, I found we were related by marriage. Her husband was my second cousin and they lived only two miles from us. This is incredible, considering the size of Alaska!

I knew full well that finding these relatives in Alaska was due to a spiritual 'visit' from my Mother who had passed on many years before.

It had been around Christmas; I was home alone sobbing, feeling lonesome, missing family. Unexpectedly there was a sense of movement in the room with no physically apparent reason. My mother immediately came to mind. It seemed like she was in the room. I felt comforted.

It also felt strange, but I remembered my beloved Grandma Gibson saying to me there is so much more in the unseen world than in the seen world which we do not recognize.

Meeting this cousin was shortly after my mother's "visit." It sure seemed my mother had something to do it.

While visiting these long lost relatives I learned that for a short time this cousin lived with us and bounced me on his knee when I was a baby.

Upon hearing my story about Hawaii and my concern for my friend, he made it possible for us to stay a week in a beautiful, very comfortable condominium in Maui right on the beach—free!

Amazing answers can come seemingly out of the blue! Only a short time before, I did not know of my cousin's existence and, in the over 600,000 miles in the largest state in the union, we met and found one another!

I flew alone, ahead of my friend, taking a less expensive "triangle flight" from Anchorage to Seattle, then California and Hawaii. It was a long but enjoyable experience.

Landing alone on Oahu I felt ecstatic from the intoxicating scent of flowers, the ocean's brilliant blue-green, and just being in Hawaii. Not having someone to share this moment was difficult. It was tempting to run up and hug a stranger! Instead, I took an island plane from Oahu to the island of Hawaii to meet and stay with Mildred Carter.

The only thing we knew about each other was we had Reflexology in common. Then we learned we had both been Unity students since childhood, were interested in holistic health, and we immediately hit it off. We talked a lot. She was younger than I'd expected, plus a lot of fun.

Mildred was not giving classes at the time. Instead she gave me personal instruction, plus we traded Foot Reflexology sessions. What an unexpected, treasured experience! And she affirmed my intuitive system with Reflexology which I had developed from techniques learned in workshops in Alaska, reading *Healing Yourself With Foot Reflexology* which Mildred authored, and my experiences with clients.

Mildred drove me all the way around the island of Hawaii, visiting her friends along the way. At fruit stands we bought delicious fruit including strawberry papayas.

Memories of this two week visit include:

- Eating sweet cherry tomatoes growing wild by the hundreds on her property.

- Helping with final move-in projects such as assembling a bookshelf.

- A cockatiel in the living room where I slept, awaking me each morning.

- The beautiful variety of finches in a massive cage covering an entire end of Lanai.

Maui Experience

After experiencing two memorable weeks on the island of Hawaii I flew to Maui for another week.

Stepping the first time into the condominium, I suddenly felt overwhelmed with feelings of joy and "coming home;" tears of happiness flowed. It felt my soul had lived here eons ago. No wonder I had wanted to go to Hawaii since childhood.

The condominium, right on the beach, had a magnificent view of the ocean and several islands! After a few days of solitude in this heavenly place on earth, my friend arrived along with a friend of hers. After the first several days alone, I was grateful for their company and eager to share the Hawaiian experience.

Touring Maui we saw beautiful gardens of orchids plus a home that had been Charles Lindbergh's. Most of all I loved being on the sandy beach, swimming in the exquisite warm water of the ocean!

We were enlivened and renewed!

One of Two Other Trips to Hawaii

The following experience took place after we had left Alaska, taken a year's sabbatical, served in Unity churches in Topeka, Kansas, and then Omaha, Nebraska.

An enormous celebration took place in Omaha, Nebraska, thanks to our daughter Kim and many others, for Don's and my 30th wedding anniversary. It included many wonderful, meaningful surprises including my dear friend, MariLyn Richardson, and Don's sister, Patricia Hutto, flying in from other states to be in our Renewal of Vows ceremony, given by our dear friend Reverend Christopher Chenoweth.

At our reception we were surprised by a gift of a Money Tree from family, congregants and other friends. Everyone was so generous that there was enough to paid for our stay in Maui.

Planning for that anniversary celebration in Hawaii included Don and our long time friend Reverend Bob Wasner, then minister at one of the Unity Churches on Oahu. The plan was for Don to speak at this church one Sunday while we were there. Because of that, Bob told his friend Wally Amos ("Famous Amos") about this anniversary trip.

While on the island of Oahu, and before heading to the Maui condominium, we had the privilege of staying in the lovely guest house of Wally and Christine Amos, who were such gracious hosts and welcomed us so lovingly!

What a thrill! We not only got acquainted with this couple while staying in a glorious setting with beautiful Hawaiian landscaping; we were also served "Famous Amos" cookies, baked for us in Wally's own oven!

The Sunday Don spoke at this Unity Center we were treated once again to an awesome, surprise anniversary celebration from the congregation.

This amazing Hawaiian trip simply started as an idea spoken aloud into being.

Our words have power! Speak the ideas that come from your desires, with power!

Opportunity to Write Your Aha's: Chapter 4

Chapter 5

Meeting Ministry's Monthly Bills...
Faith Focused Using Post-It Notes

Eager to return to ministry after our year of sabbatical in Arizona, we moved to Topeka, Kansas, to serve, and to be near Unity Village, Missouri.

A few years later we were invited to serve in a Unity church in Omaha, Nebraska. While working in the Omaha church, I completed my Licensed Unity Teacher certification. Don had worked many years in each church teaching credit classes to train Licensed Unity Teachers.

Even though I was his first Licensed Unity Teacher to graduate, he was still very supportive when I was guided instead to begin an interactive Sunday experience in Bellevue, Nebraska.

After checking with others, I found there was a definite interest in the type ministry that was my passion. I personally rented, at a nominal fee, clubhouse space in an apartment complex and announced the start of this new Unity endeavor.

Enthusiastic participants' donations helped pay part of this cost. After several weeks it felt time to find a larger, more permanent space where it would no longer be necessary to cart items in and out for every gathering.

Excited to find a great space of 900 square feet in downtown Bellevue, Nebraska, I let people know that to begin I would take responsibility for paying the increased cost of rent and utilities. I did not want anyone to feel pressure or be scared off since the cost for this facility would be close to $1,000 a month and, as yet, there were not many participants to absorb the costs.

Surprised and disappointed, I found most of those earlier participants did not show up at this new location even though it was only a couple of miles' difference. With hindsight, perhaps it was because it was my idea to move, not theirs.

However, new people, enthusiastic about what we were doing, began to attend. Since the large numbers of people expected did not materialize, I continued paying most of the cost.

This high expense required even more concentration on my thoughts and feelings, practicing staying in the High Watch of spiritual consciousness, and holding to faith in Principle and Source.

Many attendees were already tithers (see chapter 9 for more on the concept of tithing). Others began to tithe after hearing my personal beginning tithing experience and gaining their own understanding of Prosperity Principles.

The number of active participants in this ministry remained small and I began to be concerned about the finances.

Understanding that worry can block expected good, I opened for an answer during meditation. Post-Its became my friends, and my "how-to" answer. I used them to release worry about the bills, to center myself and visualize in Faith the support desired.

On each "Post-It" was written:

```
                 TYG
Next item due:   _____
Amount due:   $_____.___
Date due:        __/__/____
                 TYG
```

- TYG (Thank You God) at top and bottom! This reminded me first of all that our prosperity is not from people. Although grateful to the givers, this was a reminder that our financial good comes not from people, but from Source, which can never be depleted.

- Next item due: (rent or utilities or other)

- Amount due: (exact amount due)

- Date due: A few days earlier than the actual due date giving a feeling of breathing space.

A hardcopy of the "Post-It" was placed on my paper calendar at that same date.

Upon paying each bill, a new "Post-It" was immediately created for the next item due.

I served as Spiritual Leader of this ministry for three years; then was guided to apply for ministerial school at Unity Village, Missouri, and subsequently moved to Lee's Summit, Missouri.

During the three years serving in this Alternative Ministry I watched with amazement and gratitude how well this technique worked!

Even though the number of people remained small, enough money came in for *every* bill to be paid on time every month, all three years.

This experience proved that a ministry's income does not depend on the number of people involved, but on the focus of the leadership!

As **leaders of ministries,** practicing daily self observation of thoughts and feelings, with loving kindness in dealing with our human fears, and focusing on Spiritual Principle, we help our ministry Prosper Anyway. Our unwavering example inspires and helps those we serve, so everyone and the ministry prospers.

Ministers and spiritual leaders of ministries usually have a heavy load of activities and responsibilities. It takes an extra measure of daily dedication and resolve for a dedicated time each day, to evolve our personal spiritual understanding and a deeper awareness of our abundance.

We can learn to focus on ministerial duties, while at the same time practicing continual awareness of Inner Guidance. This often seems impossible, but is imperative for a prosperous ministry.

Prosperity comes in many forms.

In 1993, through an extensive application process, I was accepted into ministerial school at Unity Village, Missouri. A short time before, I'd been told of exciting changes planned at that time for the school. They so resonated with me that, after much prayer, I applied.

Don and I planned to maintain our residence in Omaha so he could continue his work there. Our intention was to find an inexpensive apartment for me in Lee's Summit near the school and to travel back and forth to see each other as often as possible.

As we prepared to look for an apartment, a long time friend, Unity minister, and a favorite teacher, Ed Rabel, invited me to rent his second efficiency apartment for a very low cost. I accepted, and it was considerable help to be able to pay school costs, and for two households.

It was a tiny apartment, but just right for my requirements for those short years. It was a special kick having a Murphy bed that would fold up into the wall which created space for the living room. A bonus was living across from this legend in the Unity Movement.

A very special thrill was sitting across from our daughter, Kimberly A. J. Giacometti, in ministerial class! We had each decided, unknown to the other, to apply to ministerial school the same year. Both were accepted— the first ever mother and daughter in the same class!

In our second year, Don was invited to become a faculty member at Unity School. We sold our home and moved to a larger rental apartment in Kansas City, Missouri.

In the autumn of 1994, walking along paths in the woods at Unity Village, I was inspired to live my dream ministry. In January, 1995, my Alternative Prayer Ministry became official.

In June, 1995, Kim and I, along with our classmates, graduated and were ordained as Unity ministers.

Opportunity to Write Your Aha's: Chapter 5

Chapter 6

Lake Home: A Decision and Inner Guidance

Eager to purchase a home to include a separate space for my ministry, we began looking in outlying areas of Kansas City that were convenient for Don's drive to Unity Village, yet in a country setting.

A long time desire surfaced for us to live at a lake. It was strong, so I decided this was that time. We had both grown up in the majestic Puget Sound area in Washington State. I had lived in Bremerton, Don in Seattle, and we loved living near water!

After this decision, with specific Inner Guidance, I borrowed a neighbor's newspaper for the real estate ads. It was the only resource we used.

There was a two level home for sale on a small lake in Belton. It sounded perfect in every way—except the price was out of our range. Doing some Possibility Thinking, I talked Don into viewing it. We made an appointment with a real estate agent.

Stepping into this home, we fell in love with its space and beauty. It was winter. As we looked out the dining room window onto the snowy landscape of the trees, fenced backyard and lake, a Canada Goose flew in for a landing, gliding along the icy lake. A thrill for us nature lovers! It was as if the realtor had staged it. We were both ready to move in.

The owner and realtor saw how perfect this home would be for our purposes and wanted us to have it. They worked with us for the financing, making it possible. We lived there for seven wonderful years.

Opportunity to Write Your Aha's: Chapter 6

Chapter 7

Desire To Simplify and Wow!
Paying Attention, With Willingness To Change

We began wanting a simpler life after seven years of upkeep on this older home, lawn care, and helping neighbors with the shared lakefront property.

In the summer of 2003, we visited Don's elderly mother, Lucille, now living in a lovely Seattle special care home.

We were invited to stay that week with Ken Breen, father of a good friend, Karen Breen James. Don and I had known Ken since we were teenagers in the Seattle and Bremerton, Washington, Youth of Unity teen groups. He and his wife had welcomed about twenty or so of us several times over the years to stay for a weekend at their lake place.

Now, staying in Ken's lovely north Seattle home, overlooking beautiful Puget Sound, we were able to have a precious visit one last time with Don's mother before she passed.

One morning on Ken's Lanai, feeling "in heaven" with the view and scent of the Sound, I had a strong inner pull for us to move back to this area. This was unexpected since, with all the trips made for visits over many years, I had not felt this way. My guidance was to keep silent about it in order to listen to what Don might say. Within ten minutes Don said the exact words… wanting us to move back to this area.

In recent months we had heard of a possible huge change at Unity School, releasing faculty to hire others. Don had been promised he would not be one of those released; yet we felt an uncertainty. After returning from our summer visit to Seattle in 2003, Don's job, along with all the others, ended. The school was in a major transition.

Fortunately, he was eligible to take retirement pay, qualifying by only two weeks. Whew! What a blessing that was.

We decided to sell our home in Belton, Missouri, and move to our beloved Puget Sound in Washington. It was just sooner than expected. We were invited to stay with dear friends Karen Breen James and her husband, Steve, rent free for six months in their lovely Kingston home while looking for a place to buy. This was a huge help financially, plus it was a very comfortable apartment-like space.

Finding a home to buy in this area was having disappointing results. One day close to the end of our six month stay, Don said he wanted me to see a home for rent. He had gone there with Karen to help measure a large piece of furniture. The present tenant was moving out.

While meeting the landlord, Don was told they were planning not to rent it again unless we wanted it.

I told Don "No." I still wanted to buy our own place and was not interested in seeing a rental. He persisted and described it to me. Finally I agreed to see it.

Then I saw why Don had persisted! It was a small two-bedroom mother-in-law house, with a large Redwood deck that went across the back of the house. It overlooked upper and lower yards. There were multiple flower and vegetable gardens with trails through them, plus most of the five acres was wooded.

This property was serene, beautiful, and inviting. It was owned by Jay and Judy whose home was next door. These dear people were also Unity students and offered it to us at a reduced cost.

We were so excited about the possibility of living there that the first time we talked to Jay and Judy we forgot to mention we had a small dog, LilBear, our beloved Laso-Chow mix. Concerned, we wondered if they would still accept us as renters.

Returning for our second discussion to tell them we did want to rent, we apologized, telling them that we honestly had forgotten to mention LilBear. They weren't sure about having a dog on their property until we introduced them to her. They accepted all three of us and we were thrilled and grateful.

We lived there several years, making it possible to achieve our desire of living simply. Home maintenance, yards, large areas of flower gardens were all taken care of for us. Our "Garden Cottage" was heaven on earth!

Here, amidst this peaceful setting in the woods, we were only ten minutes from the quaint towns of Kingston and picturesque Poulsbo, a worldwide tourist attraction, both on Puget Sound. We bought kayaks and enjoyed both bays. Best of all our landlords became dear friends.

Prosperity often looks different for each of us, depending on preferences for how we want to live, and can change at different times in our lives. No one is able to accurately judge whether another person is demonstrating prosperity—and it is none of our business!

Earlier we had owned large homes when our children lived at home. Now we rented a simple two bedroom cottage. We were grateful to be experiencing such abundance in the way we most wanted to live.

Opportunity to Write Your Aha's: Chapter 7

Chapter 8

Letting Go Good for Greater Good
Acting on Unexpected Message

August 1, 2008, my beloved husband and best friend passed on. I felt devastated! We had been married close to 47 years, together 50 years, meeting thanks to the Youth of Unity when we were not quite 16.

Three months after Don's passing my only sibling, my beloved sister Cathryn, passed. Our parents had passed many years before. Shortly after Cathryn, my sweet dog, LilBear, 13, who had been having severe health issues, had to be put to sleep.

When we moved to our Garden Cottage, Don and I had no idea of these pending deaths. Here I was in deep grief, yet being so well cared for, my home and personally, by dear friends, including Teresarose Keller who moved in to help. This was the perfect place for me to be living during these monumentally unwelcome changes.

In November 2010, two years into my grief healing process, while walking in my yard on a cool, beautiful, sunny day, I experienced feelings of bliss and gratitude for the beautiful area where I lived.

In the next moment, totally unexpected and out of the blue, I heard within me the words: "It's time to begin releasing this property." Silently I yelled "NO!" knowing it was a serious sign of changes to come.

Several days later my landlord, while sitting at my dining room table visiting, said, "Time is getting close to release my job as landlord." He did not know what I had "heard" only three days before. This time it was even stronger. Silently I yelled, "NOOO!"

Asking Jay when that would be he said a year to five years. First in my mind I went to five years...then to two years, determining to remain in the Puget Sound area. However, no area resonated.

One day the idea came to return to Missouri and live at a specific place. That thought brought a positive, exciting energy—and it would be only one hour from where my daughter and granddaughter lived!

The next month, December, I was in Saint Joseph, Missouri, for Christmas with my awesome daughter, Kim, and sweet baby granddaughter, Emily. In addition, I visited with a long time friend who had been a favorite teacher years ago for Licensed Teacher classes at Unity Village, Reverend Jane Waddington, who now lived in the area. While staying there overnight I experienced a definite inner knowing of "Yes, this is where I am to move."

In March 2011, only a few months after the inner message of the impending move, I flew to Missouri. On March 10, 2011, the moving van and my car arrived at my new home. Now living in a lovely two-bedroom, two-bath townhouse with a patio, there was an even more supportive community with more people nearby.

Here, continuing to move through the healing grief process, I have received phenomenal support. Passion for my ministry of serving individuals, especially ministers for spiritual and self-care, through my Alternative Unity Ministry has continued over the years.

Due to this latest move, my ministry expanded, giving me an answer for continuation of this vital work even past my lifetime. In January, 2013, on the first day the Health and Wholeness Ministry Team of Unity Worldwide Ministries was established, I was invited and accepted the position of Chair.

Best of all is living a short distance from my beloved daughter and granddaughter—so much better than flying in to visit only two or three times a year. Regularly seeing them is allowing a beautiful bond to grow with my young granddaughter. And I continue to enjoy visits with my loving son, Jeff, who lives in Arizona.

All these tremendous blessings resulted in being willing to make an originally unexpected, unwanted move. I am in my right place for now, grateful, contented.

It is always the right move when we trust and courageously follow our Intuitive Knowing, Divine Guidance. It only takes moving forward one day at a time, continuing to "listen."

Often we cannot fathom the greater blessings in store for us...until we open to possibilities. We must be willing, or at least be willing to become willing, to follow Spirit.

Opportunity to Write Your Aha's: Chapter 8

Chapter 9

Oh No, Not That!
The Key to Every Prosperity Experience

A tithe is money given freely to people and organizations who provide you with spiritual support. Giving to social service organizations is commendable; however, it is not a tithe.

Tithing is not a "bargaining tool."

A true tithe is 10% of our income. At the beginning this can seem huge. It felt that way at first for me. Later it seemed very small, especially after experiencing the results.

If you are not ready to give 10% of your entire income you can start as I did giving from a smaller portion of your income.

Using universal manifestation laws has brought me into the consciousness of permanent prosperity…not how I perceived it would happen…but here I am with so much to be grateful for!

My prosperity journey began with one major step, before we became Unity ministers, while Don and I were living in Dayton, Ohio.

After serving in the Army at Fort Huachuca, Arizona, Don was hired as a computer programmer by the National Cash Register company in Dayton, Ohio.

We, and our 11 months old daughter, Kimberly, were flown to Dayton. Later our son Donald Jeffrey "Jeff" was born there and I was a stay-at-home mom.

After seven years in Ohio we wanted to move closer to family and return to the West Coast. We had been living "high on the hog" so to speak, having a higher income and for the first time using credit cards. We used them well! Well, not well...just used them...a lot! Now in debt, we had gotten carried away spending more than was wise. There was no apparent way to afford a move.

And then everything changed one Sunday. Reverend Bette DeTurk, our Unity minister, gave an in-depth lesson that included an understanding behind the Prosperity Principle of tithing. I "got" it; however, Don did not. Don was not interested in tithing 10% of our already strapped income. As the only bread winner he felt a heavy responsibility to his family for our finances. I can imagine he thought as many do upon hearing the word "tithing":

"Oh, No! Not That!"

However I took it to heart, opening in meditation to possibilities for what I could do. This led to tithing the only money I personally received, my household money for groceries.

After three months of this spiritual practice, things dramatically changed. With no effort on Don's part, General Electric contacted Don offering a job as Systems Analyst. It was the exact kind of computer work he had wanted and came with a large salary increase.

General Electric moved us to Phoenix, Arizona, all moving expenses paid, including moving our mobile home and its two add-on rooms! Seeing the powerful results of the Tithing Principle Don began to tithe.

Underlying every one of the above stories, including my now permanent prosperity, was this consciousness of tithing.

Yes, ministries receiving tithes do benefit with a greater ability to function and serve. Isn't that what we want for places where our spiritual growth is supported?

Individuals and businesses who *freely* tithe find that you cannot out-give Spirit! Amazing, unprecedented benefits result as we act from an Understanding Faith.

Benefits of tithing include:

• assisting us in living from our Spiritual Nature and unfolding in consciousness as we put God / Spirit / our Spiritual Nature first in every area of our life, including our finances.

• gaining a keener awareness for wise use of our money and understanding that *credit card debt is not living prosperously.*

• opening to unlimited flow of Universal Substance and permanent prosperity.

• gaining the ability to live our truest desires.

• giving us the ability to bless our world.

Jim Rosemergy, in *Even Mystics Have Bills To Pay...Balancing A Spiritual Life And Earthly Living*, 2000, wrote:

Tithing is primarily "... an attitude of God first. When we live life in this way, we are blessed immensely. This is why people who tithe prosper. It is not because of the money they give, but because they put Spirit first in their lives in numerous ways. We can determine if God is first in our lives by looking at what we do with our time and money.

"When God is first, we give time to knowing God and serving Spirit by helping others and by being involved in the uplifting of the consciousness of our planet. We pray; we meditate; we study Truth [Universal Principles]. To give 10 percent of our time to these endeavors is just, for God is our creator and sustainer.

"Giving 10 percent of our income to support the unfoldment of spirituality on our planet seems fair. God is our Source. All that we have comes from this storehouse. When we know this, God is first, and we act out of this spiritual realization. It is one thing to know it intellectually; it is another to live our lives based upon this Truth and to do the work that Spirit guides us to do.

"Logically, 10 percent may seem just to you, also, but if you have never tithed before, this may seem too much. If this is the case, start at 1 percent of your income. It can be before or after taxes. It doesn't matter - just begin. Then each month increase your giving until you reach 10 percent."

"As you progress monthly ... At some point, you will conclude 'I cannot do this ... The ends will not meet if I tithe."

"How untrue ... "

"As we recommit to putting Spirit first [that fear] ... becomes a bridge to a deeper spiritual life and more prosperous and secure living." (Pages 65-66)

In the book, *Association of Unity Churches International...Its Beginning, Its Evolution, Its Vision for Worldwide Service*, it is stated that:

"Dr. Catherine Ponder has become a living legend in Unity, across New Thought and beyond for her 'rags to enrichment life' as an author and minister of a worldwide ministry. The principles she embraced and built on for more than fifty years of ministry speak volumes.

"She began tithing faithfully when 10% of her weekly income (as a secretary) was only $2.50. All these hugely successful years later she can attest with utter assurance that the simple act of putting God first financially seems to supersede and encompass all the other prosperity laws, even as important as they are individually.

"The ripple effect of her dedication to walking her talk touches the lives of millions who reach out to Unity and New Thought ministries for spiritual nurture." (Page 185)

Opportunity to Write Your Aha's: Chapter 9

Chapter 10

Ministries Can Prosper Anyway!
For Ministers and Anyone Concerned with Church Finances

Methods shared here are how Don and I helped each ministry we served prosper. This included moving three ministries that began in the red into the black.

Ministries we served:

- Port Angeles, Washington
- Anchorage, Alaska
- Topeka, Kansas
- Omaha, Nebraska
- Unity Renewal Ministries
  (my Alternative Unity Ministry)

1st: Don and I personally tithed which set the consciousness not only for our lives, but was also an example of the Tithing Principle for the Board of Trustees and congregants.

2nd: The Board of Trustees were taught and encouraged to personally use the Tithing Principle.

3rd: Whenever ministry bills were paid the tithe was paid first.

4th: Prosperity Principles were taught in Sunday services and classes.

5th: Staff and anyone working with church finances were given personal attention to develop a keen understanding of Prosperity Principles. This included focusing attention on the True Source, with gratitude to the givers and seeing them blessed, rather than focusing on the numbers of congregants or donation amounts.

6th: Thank you notes for tithes and donations were regularly sent each giver.

7th: Every incoming bill and outgoing check was blessed with appreciation and love by the bookkeepers.

It is not effective to have someone who does not support, or acknowledge, the benefits of tithing handle the money that comes into the church. It is important that the people who handle the money hold the vision for the church. Recognize the Spiritual Principle of putting God first in <u>every</u> area of your life.

Two of our awesome Unity of Anchorage staff testify to the effectiveness of Prosperity Principles. Reverend Matthew Long, our accountant before becoming a Unity Minister, said:

"We put tithing first. When we created the financial report, tithing was the first line item. God first, then people, and the rest takes care of itself."

MariLyn K. Richardson, Office Manager, before becoming a Licensed Unity Teacher, said:

"When I sat down to count the money, it was always with a sense of anticipation and joy. Each entry I made was an opportunity to give thanks for and to bless the prosperity of the giver.

"Watching the income expand was a delight, for it meant the givers were prospering and that their understanding of the Laws of Prosperity was evolving. I felt greatly blessed in that position."

~ ~ ~ ~ ~

The longer I spend writing *Prosper Anyway* the more experiences I remember and want to share, and of course prosperity experiences continue, though I must stop sometime for publishing.

Opportunity to Write Your Aha's: Chapter 10

_____

_____

_____

_____

_____

_____

_____

_____

_____

_____

_____

_____

_____

_____

_____

_____

_____

_____

_____

_____

_____

_____

_____

_____

_____

_____

_____

_____

Chapter 11

Permanent Prosperity is Possible... Even Now!

What does it mean to experience "permanent prosperity"?

What does it mean to you?

Is prosperity not having to worry about debt or money?

How do you most want to live now?

What would be most meaningful, satisfying, and fulfilling?

In Sacred Quiet times listen to your heart-mind to connect with your true desires.

- - - - -

In *Spiritual Economics* Eric Butterworth says:

"True prosperity is...determining what our souls require in order to cause them to unfold more of God; and then how to harmonize their expression with the needs of our fellow human beings so that all are benefited and inspired to unfold and express more of their inner spiritual resources." (Page 27)

Permanent prosperity often looks different for each of us and may vary in each stage of our lives.

My heart began yearning to "Live Simply, Serve Powerfully," a motto I began employing in the 1990s.

Continuing to open to this possibility my "aha's" guided me in how to live more and more in this desired life step-by-step.

Michael Beckwith says, in his book *Life Visioning*, (reproduced in a 2013 issue of Unity Magazine) that:

- "Stage one is Victim Consciousness, blaming our circumstances on people and things outside ourselves.

- "Stage two is Manifestor Consciousness, using laws of manifestation to acquire things.

- "Stage three is the beginning of a consciousness of 'living in the zone.'

- "Stage four is a state of oneness with Source while fully participating in life as a human. "

Paul Hasselbeck, in *Heart-Centered Metaphysics*, says that:

"…true prosperity is …about obtaining a consciousness through and from which Substance will flow, and ultimately about unfolding more and more Christ Consciousness. Prosperity is also the abundance of every good thing our heart desires; it originates in and from the Truth of What we are (Christ or Divine Mind), the Source of all good. Prosperity is manifested in our lives through our enlightened use of Divine Ideas. When we consciously work with these Ideas and use them wisely and lovingly, bountiful blessings will flow into our lives. As our awareness of the Infinite Substance and Supply that is perpetually available to us increases, our prosperity demonstrations will also increase. Our every desire will be abundantly satisfied in the most appropriate and fulfilling ways." (Page 365)

You are encouraged to read *Heart-Centered Metaphysics* for the finer details, including your Twelve Powers to enhance and grow your spiritual understanding for a fulfilling life.

Honest evaluation of where you are, right now, in both understanding and manifestation of good, will help you to know your next steps. Be easy on yourself and with loving kindness move forward, one step at a time. Continue this work with patience, perseverance, and courage, with trust in yourself, and in Spiritual Principles. You are worth it!

Opportunity to Write Your Aha's: Chapter 11

_____
_____
_____
_____
_____
_____
_____
_____
_____
_____
_____
_____
_____
_____
_____
_____
_____
_____
_____
_____
_____
_____
_____
_____
_____
_____
_____
_____
_____
_____
_____

Chapter 12

Release Your Success Power!
Seven Prosperity Keys and Practices

Note from author

Studying the following Universal Truth Principles until I accepted them in intellect and feeling nature, then practicing them, along with conscious Self Talk, led me into living a life of abundance.

If you are already a practicing Truth student, perhaps these ideas will be reminders that support you in your continuing journey for a greater prosperity.

If you are new to these ideas it may be helpful to begin using only one or two ideas to which you are drawn. As you feel ready, continue adding more of the practices. Further support and information can be found through Unity churches, ministries and websites.

Take one step, one day at a time, persevere and with gratitude notice each small step you gain.

This is an exciting, fulfilling, lifelong journey. Know as you move forward in this spiritual work, you bless not only yourself but our world.

Be courageous in your spiritual journey and above all treat yourself with patience and loving kindness. You are worth it!

Key Principles and Practices

1. You Are Worthy!
2. Order
3. Affirmative Prayer and Meditation
4. Visualization and Imaging
5. Self Talk
6. Forgiveness
7. Gratitude

1. Key Principle: You Are Worthy!

You (and every person) are born worthy, a spiritual being in a human body capable, and complete.

Understanding and acceptance of this Truth is key to living well. A meditation practice and prayer help!

Accept, love and value yourself. The more you do, the kinder and more loving you also are to others, and blessings can flow more freely into your life.

A new thought pattern, an affirmation to repeat often, with great feeling:

I love, accept and respect myself!

Many people with prosperity issues, when coming for spiritual counseling, have poor self-worth. Practice valuing yourself, knowing you are worthy just because you are alive! Nothing can change this about you. The more we understand and accept this Truth, the more we act out of this knowing; then we experience abundant blessings in our lives and radiate them into the world.

Self Love: A Practice

Affirm many times each day, with enthusiasm, until you feel it:

I love and accept myself just the way I am!

Mirror Work…A Simple Practice for Significant Change

You can significantly experience greater self worth with this potent practice and see positive changes begin to happen in every aspect of your life. This includes financially.

HOW-TO STEPS

In a mirror look into your eyes and repeatedly tell yourself "I love and accept you just the way you are!" Repeat this step multiple times during the day. The more uncomfortable this is, the more important it is to do, and the greater positive changes you open yourself to experience.

Continue the mirror practice daily until you notice that you have accepted this new thought pattern ... and you feel it to be true. It has been said it takes twenty-one days to create a new habit. Be willing to continue as long as it takes.

You will find it is worth the effort!

Further details on mirror work and more, including effective affirmations and meditations, can be found in *You Can Heal Your Life* by Louise Hay and on her website at www.LouiseHay.com.

The idea of positive self worth was also expressed by my beloved mother, Louise Teel. When I was a young child, she put a full length mirror in my bedroom and told me words to this effect. When looking at yourself in the mirror, appreciate and love yourself. It made a world of difference for me, a positive difference in my life. Isn't this an important idea for any child!

2. Key Principle: Order

Order, it has been said, is really the first Spiritual Principle. In following this Principle, we place our spirituality first in every area of our lives, including finances.

As we become aware of and follow our intuitive inner nudges, we experience the flow of Divine Order in beneficial ways.

A practice of placing attention first within on Spirit in everything we do, we find we are supported and led into our highest good, which also always blesses our world.

Living from Spirit first brings great joy, much more than anything in the outer can.

Finances

Practices used with finances to prosper:

Tithing.

Paying bills on time and with gratitude for what each represent, such as the electric bill for warmth and or/lighting. Vrle Minto, teacher extraordinaire, used to say he was "investing" in the utility companies. If you have Auto Pay from your bank or credit union, remember doing this in another way.

Blessing all incoming and outgoing finances…sending them off with love and appreciation.

Keeping financial records current.

Credit debt is not living prosperously, Except for necessary home and auto payments. Prosperity is living without debt.

When noticing any financial concerns, refocus on Source, then do whatever is required to best take care of business.

"But strive first for the kingdom of God, and his righteousness, and all these things will be given to you as well." (Matthew 6:33 NRSV)

3. Key Principle: Affirmative Prayer

<u>Benefits</u>

The Unity way of prayer that we find most effective is not praying "to God" nor "asking" for something. Instead, we pray "from a *consciousness*" of God, with an awareness of Source.

When we pray from this consciousness, affirming absolute Truth over apparently limiting "facts," it is from a place of power, creativity and peace.

Affirmative Prayer includes both Truth Denials and Affirmations. Correctly used these tools uplift our consciousness into a greater awareness of our higher spiritual nature and opens us to making positive changes in our lives.

We all experience times of fear and worry; however, through using Principles of Truth Denials and Affirmations, we have ability to diffuse the power we are giving to fear and worry and change our focus to experience our Faith, confidence, and answered prayer.

The power of choice is always ours. Be aware when fear and lack thoughts enter, rather than giving them power, acknowledge them in your mind then refocus on where you want your power to focus on Spirit. It is your belief system, your consciousness, that makes positive change possible.

Deborah Shouse, in a November/December 2013 *Unity Magazine* article titled "Prospering During the Spiritual Journey," quotes Victoria Moran as saying:

[Prosperity is the] "… freedom not to have to worry about money." (Page 37)

I would add that it is having what is truly needed in perfect timing. Elise Cowan affirms this in her article the "Third Day of Lent" published in Silent Unity's 2016 Lent booklet *Higher Ground*:

"In quiet contemplation, we are guided to our highest good through the still, small voice within us. As we turn our attention to the wisdom of God in us, our way is made clear. We follow our inner guidance and seeming miracles occur.

"Responding to divine direction, we experience the abundance of God's good. As we acknowledge this good in our lives, it grows." (Page 10)

Truth Denials

What they are:

Paul Hasselbeck, in *Heart-Centered Metaphysics, says* "[A Truth] Denial is not the mere wishing or hoping something will go away, nor is it the withholding of comfort or happiness." (Page 215)

It is used to evolve consciousness into alignment with Spiritual Law [Principle].

Correctly used, Truth Denials help us to deny that the "facts" have power in our life. They help us to stop resisting the flow of good that is so natural throughout our lives.

It is our ability to release the energy and power we have invested in believing the negative/error thoughts, feelings and beliefs.

Truth Denials are forms of prayer that:

- make it is easier to focus on "Practicing the Presence"

- assist us in continuing to expand our consciousness of abundance

- help keep our focus on what we most desire

This process diffuses the energy and power we have given to negativity.

Why and how Truth Denials and Affirmations work is detailed in books by Linda Martella-Whitsett, *Divine Audacity*, and Paul Hasselbeck's *Heart-Centered Metaphysics*

These books help give a clear understanding of these two powerful tools and enhance your ability to prosper.

HOW-TO STEPS

Speak denials as though you were **gently** sweeping away cobwebs, so as to not add power to the negative.

Always follow with an Affirmation of Truth.

Correct use of a Truth Denial cleanses our mind of error beliefs, leaving room to rebuild our consciousness through Truth Affirmations. These processes affect both mind and heart and allow us to move forward into the life we desire.

Examples:

In *How to Pray Without Talking To God* Martella-Whitsett says:

"I set aside any concern about my well-being right now, refusing any resting place in my awareness for worry and fear. I shush compulsive worry ... I refuse to indulge in another moment of apprehension about this situation." (Page 101)

According to Reverend Claudell County, in *Learning to Let Go,* Silent Unity booklet for Lent (2015):

"When aware of any thoughts of money concerns: I give no power to thoughts of not having enough.

"I give no power to thoughts of lack.

"No thought, belief or experience has the power to limit my Spirit [and my flow of good].

"My circumstances have no power over me."

Truth Affirmations

What they are:

Affirmations, properly worded, are powerful tools for effective upliftment of consciousness. They can transform our heart-mind, and move us forward into our desired life.

They are used to raise consciousness and open us to Divine Ideas that, as we act on them, bring them into visibility.

They help to cultivate a consciousness of plenty.

They are vital to use after a Truth denial.

They are more than positive or possibility thinking and are not wishful thinking, but are anchored in solid Truth and Spiritual Principle.

The use of Truth affirmations continues to help me live more often in a higher state of consciousness— one of peace and inner knowing for abundant living.

HOW-TO STEPS

* Present tense words rather than future tense puts our power into ability to manifest in the present moment.

Poor wording: "I *will be* abundantly prospered."

Correct wording: "I *AM* abundantly prospered."

- Write in the first person: I AM …

- Short sentences (10 words or less) are best to effectively commit an affirmation to memory so it can automatically come to mind.

- Use words that engage both your mind and feeling nature.

- Speak the affirmation aloud with power and faith or, if need be, silently.

My practice, which I invite you to do, is to read Truth Affirmations and work with them several times until you experience their upliftment and inspiration.

Use affirmations that speak to you, or you may want to create your own. It can be helpful, when you feel a heightened energy from certain words you read, to use them as a part of your affirmation.

Examples

- I live in a universe overflowing with plenty for me and everyone.
(We can look around us to see it. In appreciation for this good, we attract greater good).
- All that I need comes to me in the perfect time, in the perfect way.
- The rich Substance of Spirit can never be depleted. It is eternal and unlimited.
- I use my resources with wisdom and faith.
- I AM content and remain open to new good.
- I give freely and willingly.

- I AM worthy and able to live a life of abundance.
- I claim my Divine Ideas and manifest abundance.
- I pay attention to the facts, yet focus more on the Source!
- Facts are changeable. Truth is eternal.
- The rich Substance of Spirit is unlimited, everywhere present, and available to me (to all).
- Abundance is mine and everywhere present.
- I am blessed and I give thanks!

From the Chapter on "Divine Order" in the Silent Unity booklet *Empowering Prayers for Everyday Life*:

"My mind is poised and my heart is serene, knowing [Spirit] works in all and through all to bring forth great possibilities in my life." (Page 26)

A shorter version that is easier to remember:

I am poised, serene, and move forward with ease.

And from *Daily Word* Magazine, February 5, 2015, on Inspiration.

"I affirm what is right and good, [setting] my inner world in order and a pattern of order is expressed in my life.

"As I act on my deepest inspirations the energy of Spirit pulses through me. I embrace divine ideas and pursue my dreams with great courage, certainty and faith!"

Shortened version:

I act with courage and faith.

Working with Catherine Ponder's *Dynamic Laws of Prosperity,* and her pamphlet "Decree Sheet," made a huge shift in my prosperity consciousness! (http://catherineponder.wwwhubs.com)

Following are a few of Ponder's affirmations.

- My words are charged with prospering power.

- I do not depend upon persons or conditions for my prosperity…blessing persons and conditions…amazing channels of supply are open to me now. (First a denial then an affirmation.)

- I dare to prosper now.

- I dissolve in my mind any idea that my own can be withheld from me.

- I let go worn out things, conditions, relationships. I loose and let go. Divine order is now establish.

- Vast improvement comes quickly in every phase of my life now. Every day in every way, things are getting better and better.

- I use the positive power of my Christ Mind with wisdom, love and good judgment in handling all my finances now.

Additional information on affirmations can be found in Unity publications, including *Heart-Centered Metaphysics* by Reverend Paul Hasselbeck.

Meditation

Benefits

Whatever circumstances we experience, they are met more confidently with the peace, strength and courage we gain through meditation.

Meditation also helps us stay aware of our Inner Guidance in our day to day life.

I am grateful to have known, and to know, such happiness in my life. However, the greatest joy comes through having a daily meditation practice, which I highly recommend.

There are many ways one can practice meditation. Keep it simple and find what works best for you. It can change over time.

My meditation practice includes connecting with the One Source through Practicing the Presence and quieting until I become acutely aware and focused on Divine Stillness; then I allow time to rest and *just be* in this deep Silence.

Afterwards my practice is to take this experience of peace, love and light into my day to help traverse the circumstances that make up one's human experience.

Through a daily meditation practice we connect with the ever present, eternal flow of Divine Ideas, and our imagination, power, wisdom and faith centers, to achieve what we had never believed was possible. Possibilities are then infused with Divine energy.

Neuroscientists have found that meditators, while meditating, shift their brain activity, decreasing negative effects of stress, mild depression and anxiety.

In *Healing Letters,* Myrtle Fillmore says "Those who take time regularly and who give themselves to the necessary prayer and meditation, to get new light and to round out their consciousness and ability to use all their [spiritual] faculties, find that they go from one prosperity to another." (Page 74)

Meditation is a practice, not something to get down perfectly. Let go of expectations to do it "just so." You gain in ability and in consciousness every time you meditate—even when it doesn't seem at the time that anything is happening. Go into it with a willing spirit.

Meditation can feel like coming home to oneself. What a wonderful gift to give ourselves. And we come to better know ourselves—both our divinity and our humanity.

We become more keenly aware of attitudes and beliefs we are holding which block the flow of our abundant good, and what is necessary for us to know and do to open the flow.

A meditation practice makes it possible to notice subtle inner nudges of Spirit throughout the day, guiding us to always know what to do.

When the number of tasks for the day look and feel overwhelming, meditation gives us an ability to ease into the day with serenity, and then see with clarity what is truly ours to accomplish that day.

In experiencing meditation, you will find that you seem to have more time in the day. This may include knowing when to let go of things you had planned to do, while more easily accomplishing what you need to do.

If it seems impossible to fit meditation into your busy schedule, it can help to get up a few minutes earlier. Meditation has a direct influence on our entire day. *It is worth it!*

Guidelines include: (See which of the following you find most helpful.)

- Plan ahead making it the same time daily, preferably the first thing upon awakening and before moving into the day's activities. Make it early enough so you won't feel rushed and perhaps again in the late afternoon. It doesn't have to take very long.

- Create, as best you can, a serene, uncluttered quiet space in a comfortable chair. Music that calms and centers can be helpful, or perhaps a candle, incense or smudge stick.

- Relaxation is a necessary first step. Allow tension to release, focus on your breath, allow your whole body to relax. I've found that first blowing out through the mouth, before breathing in through the nose is an excellent way to release stress.

- One way to still your thoughts is to simply, silently or aloud, tell your thoughts *be still* a few times; or focus on a sacred object or a candle, something that calms you—perhaps something in nature such as the image of a serene lake.

- Concentrating on a truth affirmation for a time, can help you to move your attention from an outer focus and more easily begin to turn your attention within to the Still Point—your still small voice.

Linda Martella-Whitsett, in *How to Pray Without Talking to God*, says:

"Concentrate on I AM affirmations that bring you into alignment with Divine Nature and your Divine Identity: I AM a rippling stream of Divine Peace." (Page 119)

The following quote by Myrtle Fillmore in *Healing Letters* tells us to:

"Be still. Be still. Be still. God in the midst of you is substance. God in the midst of you is wisdom. Let not your thoughts be given over to lack, but let wisdom fill them with substance and faith." (Page 49)

As you move into the day's activities, do so in gratitude with a consciousness of love.

It is normal to move in and out of the meditation.

As you prepare to end the meditation, allow gratitude to well up in your whole being, from the crown of your head to the tips of your toes.

Then gently move into your day, taking with you the gratitude, peace and well-being you have gained. Even when it has not been the experience desired, know that by doing a meditation practice that you, those around you, and our world, have been blessed.

Paul Hasselbeck, in *Heart-Centered Metaphysics* chapter on meditation (Pages 59-64), has a more complete set of excellent guidelines on how to meditate.

Daily prayer and meditation builds Spiritual Consciousness…allowing us to experience greater good than only looking at the facts would allow.

From *Lessons in Truth* by H. Emilie Cady (1919) as quoted in Linda Martella-Whitsett's book *How To Pray Without Talking To God*:

"Watch carefully, and you will find there are some things, even in the active [sic] unselfish doing, which would better be left undone that [sic] you should neglect regular meditation." (Page 109)

Meditation is how we can experience our Source/our Spirit in the sacred quiet as we turn within.

Each time you sit and meditate makes a positive difference for your life. This is true even when the experience does not feel like much has happened.

Through prayer and meditation we get to know and understand ourselves better, our humanity, and our Divinity. It helps us see where our thinking can be adjusted to reflect higher Truth Principles.

Each experience in the Sacred Silence increases our ability to initiate within us that which resonates with the Universal Laws of Abundance, opening us to our True Source.

Gaining a prosperity consciousness, most of all a keen awareness of our Source, is not a quick fix. It continues to develop throughout one's lifetime with our attention, intention and practice. How wonderful is that?

Each meditation invites us to center, de-stress, and be aware of inner nudges (guidance) and alert to outer signs of Spirit constantly leading us.

Sitting in the early morning, relaxed and aware, gives one an opportunity to adjust any negative thoughts and feelings and experience new energy for the day, as well as inspiring ideas, uplifted feelings and gratitude for living.

Thousands of thoughts crowd our mind constantly, so it is a blessed relief to periodically pause and focus on one thing only (perhaps on our breath) for a time, allowing us a time of rest and renewal.

Linda Martella-Whitsett in her book *How to Pray Without Talking to God* says:

"If you are not in the habit of daily prayer, reflect upon what may be in the way of your making it so. Cough up all your excuses, write each one on a scrap of paper, laugh about them, and then tear up the scraps into miniscule pieces. Dig a hole in the ground and let the scraps become fertilizer because that's all they are worth. Take a deep breath." (Page 126)

What benefits might you gain by investing in deeper aspects of daily prayer such as meditation?

Simple Sitting Meditation

A teaching I learned many years ago in Unity that is vital to one's life—no problem can be solved from the same level of consciousness that created it, such as worry or fear.

Meditation is a practice for living in a consciousness of understanding faith and power.

It is a practice ... you don't have to do it perfectly and the more you practice the greater you will experience its blessings.

There are many ways one can practice meditation. Use whatever way works best for you, and that can change over time. Keep it simple and enjoyable.

HOW-TO STEPS

- Plan ahead.
- Make time when you won't feel too busy or rushed, perhaps before the start of the activities of the day.
- A quiet area is conducive with a comfortable chair, and items near that evoke the sacred.

Relaxation is primary.

You may find these ideas helpful for relaxing:

- Acknowledge briefly, then release, thoughts of concerns and disturbing emotions remembering and affirming that the Truth within you is greater than anything in the outer.

- Focus briefly on your breath.
- It could help to simultaneously release concerns and blow out through your mouth, then breathe in deeply, attuning to Spirit within, and allowing your belly to relax...allowing your whole self to relax more deeply.

My granddaughter, Emily, at age nine, shared this fun method she learned in the Youth Ministry at Unity Church of Overland Park, Kansas:

- Blow out as if you are blowing out a candle.
- Breathe in as if you are taking in the scent of flowers.

Another way to quiet thoughts, as taught by Joseph Cornell in his book *Listening to Nature: How to Deepen Your Awareness of Nature,* is telling yourself:

- On your in breath: Still
- On your out breath: Ness
- *Continuing this breathing practice for a time, on each full breath you are telling yourself Still-Ness.* (p. 34)

Robert Brumet, author, facilitator of Mindfulness Retreats, and Unity Minister, has said that: The mind thinks...it's what it does. In meditation allow thoughts to float in and out.

Letting go resistance to them opens us to [our inner] space. (paraphrased)

It is primary to practice the Spiritual Principle of non-resistance.

Towards the end of your meditation allow gratitude to well up.

It is also a potent time to end with an affirmation such as one of the following (you may want to shorten them to make them easier to remember):

• Immersed in peace and love, I Am open and receptive to my Heart Wisdom.

• Relaxed and renewed, I trust myself and open to the continual creative flow within.

• I now confidently move forward, willing to do what is mine to do…in gratitude.

A favorite of mine which I keep where it is easy to see is:

"Relax and let go all tense, anxious personal striving. Let Divine ideas work for you." A quote from Myrtle Fillmore's book *How to Let God Help You*, reproduced in *Moments with Myrtle: A Meditation Book* by Barbara Bergen.

Goldie Hawn's prescription for inner peace in an article "Mindfulness Matters", published in *AARP Magazine*, 2015 says, "… meditation thickens the [brain] cortex where we make decisions, analyze, feel more connected to others and dream...it's essential to take time to breathe or spend a few minutes in nature away from phones and computers.

"Slow down; enjoy this ride".

Hawn shared this simple meditation:

1st. Sit with your belly softened and take three deep breaths. Now focus on breathing normally.
2nd. When thoughts arise, let them go, like clouds passing in the sky.
3rd. Be patient. Your heart rate will slow, and your stress will eventually melt away.

That article shared this simple technique, and others are being taught in schools through Goldie's MindUp program, helping children manage emotions and behavior.

The above three steps are practiced in those schools for a brain break three times a day, two minutes each time.

A significant practice of mine comes from May Rowland, Director of Silent Unity for fifty years, who was known for saying, "Through practice we can feel the Presence of God working in and through us at all times no matter what we are doing."

A sitting meditation, Practicing the Presence, gives ability to be aware of Divine Presence during the day's activities and notice the Inner Nudges from Spirit.

Then, more often in the days' activities we can experience our Sacred Peace, Love and the Guidance.

This practice then helps during the day, for ability to focus on the constant flow back and forth between the outer and inner (often called our "still small voice").

Another way to talk about our still small voice is stated very succinctly by Martha Beck in an article titled "Your Intuition Has Something to Tell You" found in the January, 2015 issue of "O Magazine", as follows:

"I won't mince words. If you've never learned to tap into your intuition, your life is almost certainly much more difficult than it needs to be. Why? Because your intuition helps you make choices based on what you actually want, it helps you avoid trouble, draws you toward positive situations and away from negative ones. It circumvents your intellect-which can tell you all kinds of inaccurate, critical, self-defeating things-and instead guides you based on what your body, your very essence, knows to be true. Your intuition never criticizes you. If you're hearing an inner voice that sounds shaming, blaming, disdainful, withering, or mean, you're not sharing your intuition, which functions more like a kitten: It may be urgent, nervous, or resistant, but it never could imply that something is wrong with you."

We can learn to listen to our intuition, with practice, first with small things. Through that practice we become very discerning about what our intuition is telling us. And, I believe it is constantly guiding each one of us—we must learn to listen.

It makes life much more interesting, fun and often easier!

We can know whatever we need to know when we need to know it.

You can find your particular way of living in both inner and outer awareness through a deep desire and by holding this intention in mind and heart.

As we remain alert to the presence within, we are able to continue moving forward in life, accomplishing our highest intentions.

Intention

First, in moments of Sacred Quiet, listen to your deepest held desire. During this time, then periodically during the day's activities, hold in your heart and mind a one-pointed focus in a specific positive direction. Relax, without any sense of coercion or force or compulsion, but with gentle concentration.

Letting go of doubts, picture that desire happening. Release wondering how it will happen…opening to "This or something better."

The beloved, late Louis Stolis, Ph.D. of Life Institute and author of *Sacred Science (Secrets and Shortcuts for Integrating Spirituality into Your Daily Life),* states that:

"The conscious mind does not know how the universe is going to manifest our intentions.

"We should not waste precious energy trying to figure out how it is going to happen. ...we simply KNOW that the Universe will create it for us.

"We understand that the whole Universe is Energy. The energy of Intention grows as it is sustained.

"Hold the feeling that Creation is manifesting [y]our desires...we need to overcome the limiting beliefs, doubts, and fears we hold. ..

"When doubt creeps in, cast it out with an affirmation, a feeling of strength...

"Doubt is just a lower vibration...look (with a) higher evaluation..simply let (the doubt) pass.

"As you engage in (this process) ...(your next move will be revealed)..Know that the inner force is so magnificent, powerful and omnipotent it will create a passion for life beyond your wildest dreams.

"*Allow* the Universe to create the circumstances and determine how the events will unfold. Trust.

"The more we trust this Energy, the more it will reveal itself to us. The revelations come at unexpected times and in various forms.

"Fortuitous events begin to happen more and more frequently. As our energy becomes higher and finer, the Universe increases its rate of response." (Page 114)

4. Key Principle: Visualization and Imaging

"I remove images from my mind and replace them with visions of abundance, love, and success."
Daily Word magazine, January 9, 2015: Reflection

We continually use our powerful, spiritual faculty of Imagination whether we are aware of it or not. We visualize future happenings, negative or positive, from a place of fear or from a centered awareness.

We manifest those thoughts we hold most in mind. Whatever we think with *conviction*, we manifest!

Through using our power of Imagination with intention we can accomplish the seemingly impossible. I know from experience!

We can manifest amazing blessings from the Universe!

HOW-TO STEPS AND PRACTICES

- As you go about your day notice what you are picturing in your mind. Is it what you want?

- Practice noticing your thoughts and images, changing any negative to positive.

- Be specific about what you want while opening to even greater good, always affirming "this or something better."

- Let go doubt, wondering how your good could happen; use your energy positively, powerfully.

- Let go need, changing neediness to preferences.

Charles Fillmore, in *Atom Smashing Power of Mind*, says, "To attain prosperity, think about prosperity, industry, and efficiency. Fill your mind to overflowing with thoughts of success; realize that the fullness of all good belongs to you by Divine right. To this add a feeling of happiness and joy and you have the recipe for abundant and lasting prosperity." (Page 105)

One of the *biggest keys* for my every manifestation has been the practice of imagining- seeing, until I 'got it' in consciousness:

Charles Fillmore, in *Dynamics for Living,* chapter on Prosperity, says, "*Be still and turn within to the great Source. See with the eye of faith that the whole world is filled with substance. See it falling all about you as snowflakes of gold and silver*.

"In laying hold of substance in the mind and bringing it into manifestation, we play a most important part. (Our) work is to express substance ideas in material form. *Identify yourself with substance until you make it yours.*" (Page 192)

While writing this chapter, I read two current authors who agree that Imagination is the most important of our twelve inherent Spiritual Gifts.

Linda Martella-Whitsett, author of *Divine Audacity*, delves deeper into understanding our Spiritual Faculty of Imagination and includes practices for our Twelve Powers.

"Imagination is our powerful capacity to picture what can be and, by holding that idea and developing it until we feel its effects while it is yet unmanifest, to live into that idea until it essentially becomes our reality. In a sense, imagination is our primary power because it is essential for the cultivation of all our magnificent spiritual capacities." (Page 77)

5. Key Practice: Self Talk

How do you talk to yourself? What is your inner talk about yourself and your life? Have you noticed that thoughts/inner talk is nearly constant?

Changing any negative "inner yammering" to positive and kind, creative self-talk reflects more of the latter into our life.

This, too, requires ongoing practice. Noticing our thoughts gives us awareness of where we could be headed and gives us the ability to change them if we prefer more positive outcomes.

Thoughts we *most hold* in mind will likely manifest.

- Be kind to yourself and your thought process. You can tell your thoughts "Be Still" (repeatedly until they quiet). Sometimes I find it works well to tell them with love and humor "shush!"

- To make this change it can help to take a deep breath while changing from a negative to a positive thought.

- Memorize a short, favorite, potent affirmation that then comes automatically into your mind whenever most helpful.

A couple of my favorites:

I love, respect and trust myself!

After accomplishing a difficult task or something I've been putting off:

I did it! I am doing it!

6. Key Principle: Forgiveness

Forgiveness is a gift we give ourself. Forgiving another, ourself, or circumstance frees us and allows us to move forward and prosper.

It may at times seem impossible. It is not! I found it can happen if we become *willing to be willing.* This can take some time—days, weeks or longer.

We can, through affirmations, prayer and meditation, open in mind and heart to the freeing love of Spirit within us. We can invite this Unconditional Love to sweep through our thoughts and emotions and do its perfect healing work.

Through forgiveness we take back our power, no longer giving it to another person or circumstance. It does not mean we allow inappropriate behavior to continue; and sometimes we find that we must stop associating with someone.

When we pay attention to self talk and our feelings, we may find a daily need to practice forgiveness, including for ourself, and to begin again.

Forgiveness of everything and everyone, including ourselves, means no longer carrying unnecessary burdens, freeing our energy for the ability to move forward in life and attract our greatest good.

A dear friend, soon after we met, told me of this experience:

His son, a young adult and only child, was riding his motorcycle when he was hit by a drunk driver and killed.

That whole night he was in deep agony and devastating grief. Then at some point during the night he experienced a healing, and an ability to forgive.

During the court appearance of the drunk driver my friend told him he forgave him. That young man, the judge, and others in the courtroom were very deeply moved. I can believe it changed that young man's life, as well as the lives of others in the courtroom.

The following ideas and affirmations are by Catherine Ponder from her many books, her *Decree* pamphlet, and now online. Working with them had a major impact on my consciousness including for my prosperity.

"Spend half an hour every day mentally forgiving everyone that you are out of harmony with, or are concerned about. Subconsciously they will respond."

"If you have accused yourself of failure or mistakes, forgive yourself, too."

"I fully and freely forgive. I loose you and let you go to your good quickly and in peace. All is cleared up between us now and forever."

"Everyone who has offended me I forgive. Whatever has made me bitter, resentful, unhappy, I forgive. Within and without I forgive. This includes myself. I forgive."

"Everyone who I ever offended forgives me. This includes everything I have done to anyone that I know about or do not know about or do not remember."

"I am forgiven by everything and everyone. I forgive and I am forgiven. All things are cleared up between us now and forever."

Speaking of forgiveness for oneself:

A great help for me over the years was being told by a spiritual teacher early in my spiritual practice that this work is a practice…it is not about perfection.

When we mess up, rather than giving ourself the guilt treatment, we can learn from the experience and start again. I am forever grateful to that teacher!

Notice I didn't say "if" we mess up but "when." Perhaps we could relate practicing living these Principles to being on a human-divine roller coaster. Remember to keep things light and enjoy the ride.

7. Key Principle: Gratitude

A heart filled with gratitude can keep expanding one's blessings.

It is a key practice that perhaps is the easiest and most enjoyable.

Noticing what there is to be grateful for, even the smallest of things, lifts us into an energy of joy and the power to create, thus expanding our blessings.

Living in an attitude of gratitude attracts amazing blessings. It allows us to be open to new ideas and ways of being and doing that blesses us and others.

The simple practice of gratitude can change our lives. Sages throughout the centuries have noted that:

As we count our blessings, they multiply.

Gratitude expands our awareness of God, to our Spirit. It opens us to appreciate and receive our good.

Whatever circumstance we are going through we can always find reasons to feel gratitude, noticing even the tiniest of reasons.

Just before sleep is an especially good time to think about the day, one's life, and to focus on gratitude.

Gratitude might include:

- A roof overhead.

- People in your life.

- The beauty in nature...seeing birds through a window or while walking outdoors, soaking up the lovely energy or enjoying the beauty of different landscaping around the neighborhood.

- Technology which expands awareness of one's world and allows you to connect with people worldwide.

- The courage in taking one step at a time to move through a challenging circumstance.

- The ability to continue growing and the freedom to practice Universal/Spiritual Principles and experience your Highest Good

- Remembering all that you have accomplished in the past few hours, your life and each new day.

Additional Awareness, Practice and Support

The more we learn about ourselves, our interior life, truly coming to know our heart-mind, the clearer the way becomes for moving creatively forward into a life of fulfillment.

Honest observation of our thoughts and feelings, with loving kindness, is a primary focus.

Other than in our own belief, there is no smaller or larger demonstration in the Absolute Realm. In Universal Principle all desires and intentions for manifestation are the same even when one seems more important than another.

It can help to start by demonstrating what feels smaller; then later, seek what seem like larger desires.

Work to Let Go

Let go belief in "size."

Let go any *need* to have your intention happen.

Do not waste energy wondering *how* it could happen.

Put your faith in Spiritual Principle, and in yourself.

Be persistent, patient, open in mind and heart and courageous in following your Inner Guidance.

Listen.   Trust.   Act.

Ability to use our spiritual faculty of Faith grows stronger each time we use and activate it, so life begins to unfold with greater ease and success.

Throughout my many years in Unity I have learned that Understanding Faith is a Divine Idea that is the perceiving power of mind coupled with the power to shape Substance. And, it is knowing that whatever good we seek is already ours in Spirit.

Martha Smock, former *Daily Word* editor, in "A Prosperity Meditation", quotes Hebrew 11:1 (KJV) which says that "Faith is the assurance of things hoped for, the conviction of things not seen." She goes on to say, "In times of lack, faith sees plenty. In times of discouragement, faith sees success and achievement. In times of frustration, faith sees fulfillment."

Our human drama:

Sometimes it helps people to hear that others have similar experiences, to know one is normal:
Even after years of growing and unfolding my spirituality, I often experience very human emotions, and grow even more as I acknowledge and work with them.

We are spiritual beings living as human beings in a human world. We are here to learn and grow.

What Helps Me Includes

It helps to have inspiration at hand like *Daily Word* magazine and Silent Unity booklets such as "Empowering Prayers for Everyday Life" to lift us as we prepare for our day, and to guide us, then bless us at day's end. They remind us of our highest Truth, plus where we want most to keep our focus. (This booklet was available as of the writing of this book. If you cannot find this particular publication, there are many inspirational booklets available through www.unity.org.)

Placing favorite affirmations where they are easily seen is also helpful, including on the refrigerator, a bathroom mirror and on the night stand to see them first thing in the morning and the last thing at night.

Be patient with yourself. Remind yourself often that you are growing in spiritual understanding; that it is an ongoing process.

It helps to periodically pause from daily activity, breathe deeply, and experience a few moments of peace.

Live more and more in calm and peace, stilling anxious thoughts, with less and less hurried behaviors.

In moments of inner peace we are able to hear Spirit guide us to what is most beneficial with the most extraordinarily wonderful timing.

Returning to the day's activities, you can practice flowing attention back and forth, from the outer to the inner, keeping in touch with your Intuitive Wisdom—Spirit. We always have the guidance we desire available to us.

A spiritual teacher once said there is truly only one decision we ever have to make—to turn within to Spirit for direction.

Keep your determination, moving forward with intention, confidence and courage, yet flexible enough to change. Remember to be patient with the process.

Enjoy a sense of humor, let go of a sense of urgency, and stay light-hearted. It makes a difference!

Keep trusting yourself, following your truest guidance, Spirit within.

Realize how blessed you are to have come as far as you have already in life. You are immensely blessed and supported by the Universe.

Opportunity to Write Your Aha's: Chapter 12
(Add your own pages, as helpful)

Commitment
(author unknown)*

"Commitment is what transforms a promise into reality.

It is the words that speak boldly of your intentions.

And the actions which speak louder than words.

It is making the time when there is none.

Coming through time after time after time, year after
*   year after year.*

Commitment is the stuff character is made of;

the power to change the face of things.

It is the daily triumph of integrity over skepticism."

* "Commonly attributed to Abraham Lincoln or Shearson Lehman.

Author's History

Growing in spiritual understanding to develop true understanding about prosperity came through Unity classes, workshops, materials and Sunday services.

This adventure began at Unity Center in Bremerton, Washington where, Reverend Marian Brown was minister. As a young child I attended Sunday School, and as a teenager participated in Youth of Unity led by Gay Raney, who was dedicated to Unity teachings and teens.

I sometimes visited the Seattle, Unity Church of Truth with my boyfriend and future husband Don Jennings. Favorite teachers there included:

Youth of Unity Sponsor, Francis Ojay
Reverends Donald O'Connor
Reverend Dorothy O'Conner (later Pierson)

In adult years my Unity ministers were Reverends:
Bette De Turk, Dayton, Ohio
Blaine Mays, Phoenix, Arizona
Grover Thornsberry, Seattle, Washington
Michael Murphy, Burien, Washington

Unity Village Chapel, Unity Village, Missouri:
Sig and Jane Paulsen
Frank and Martha Giudici

In my Continuing Education Classes my favorites included:
Jane Waddington

In 1974-2004 - I took many classes in the ministries we served, by awesome Bible and metaphysics teacher, my beloved husband, Reverend Donald R. Jennings.

My additional classes:

1980's to become a Licensed Unity Teacher in 1989

1993-95 Ministerial classes

Years before ministerial school I served with Don as Partner in Ministry serving in Unity Churches in:

- Port Angeles, Washington
- Anchorage, Alaska
- Topeka, Kansas
- Omaha, Nebraska

In 1990-93 - As a Licensed Unity Teacher, I founded, and was Spiritual Leader for an alternative Unity ministry in Bellevue, Missouri

1993-95 - I was in the Unity Ministerial program, Unity School of Christianity, Unity Village, Missouri; and graduated June 1995 plus was ordained by the Association of Unity Churches (now Unity Worldwide Ministries).

1995-2015 founded and served through Unity Renewal Ministries an Alternative Prayer Ministry providing individuals, especially Spiritual Leaders, self care support by phone, email and in person.   Now semi-retired.

Resources

Bergen, Barbara. *Moments with Myrtle*. Reprinted with
    permission of Unity Books, 2000.

Butterworth, Eric. *Spiritual Economics*, Unity Village,
    MO: Unity House, 2nd revised paperback
    edition, 1998.

Carter, Mildred. *Healing Yourself with Foot
    Reflexology*, West Nyack, NY: Parker Publishing
    Company, 1969.

Cornell, Joseph. *Listening to Nature: How to Deepen
    Your Awareness of Nature*, Nevada City, CA:
    Dawn Publications, 1987.

Fillmore, Charles. *Dynamics for Living: A Topical
    Compilation of Essential Fillmore Teachings*,
    Unity Village, MO: Unity School of Christianity,
    Charles Fillmore Reference Library, 1967.

Fillmore, Myrtle. Myrtle Fillmore's *Healing Letters*,
    Unity Village, MO: Unity School of Christianity,
    March 1978.

Hasselbeck, Paul. *Heart-Centered Metaphysics*, Unity
    Village, MO: Unity House, 2010. Used with
    permission of Unity, www.unity.org.

Martella-Whitsett, Linda. *Divine Audacity: Dare to Be
    the Light of the World*, Charlottesville, VA:
    Hampton Roads Publishing Company, Inc., 2015.

Martella-Whitsett, Linda. *How To Pray Without Talking To God...Moment by Moment, Choice by Choice,* Charlottesville, VA: Hampton Roads Publishing Company, Inc., 2011.

Mosley, Glenn R. and Dunlap, Rebekah A. *Association of Unity Churches International... Its Beginning, Its Evolution, Its Vision for Worldwide Service*, Lees Summit, MO: Association of Unity Churches International, 2006

Ponder, Catherine. *Prosperity Decrees* pamphlet, Palm Desert, FL: Self-published 1971.

Rosemergy, Jim. *Even Mystics Have Bills To Pay: Balancing a Spiritual Life and Earthly Living*, Unity Village, MO: Unity House, 2000.

Smock, Martha. "A Prosperity Meditation" reprint from *Daily Word*, Unity Village, MO: Unity School of Christianity, c1980s.

Stolis, Louis, Ph.D. *Sacred Science (Secrets and Shortcuts for Integrating Spirituality into Your Daily Life)*, Lazarus Publishing, NY: 1997.

Whaley, Harold. *Whatsoever Things Are True,* Unity Village, MO: Unity School of Christianity, 1980.

Additional support for these teachings can be found worldwide in Unity churches and ministries in classes, workshops and Sunday services, plus websites and books.

Message of Support from Carolyn

Through continuing to study, pray, meditate and take courageous action using Spiritual Principles, you, too, can *Prosper Anyway…Beyond Limitations of Low Income or World Economy*!

Trust yourself—your Inner Knowing! After all, look how far you've already come in life.

While writing these last pages this "aha" came. Using Spiritual Prosperity Principles in our personal life, we may later find that those experiences have in some way blessed our world!

Yes, prosperity is more than money and things, yet it includes these, too! As you prosper, it also lifts our world's prosperity consciousness.

I am grateful for you, the reader and glad for whatever blessings these ideas spark in you to enhance your awareness for living well.

Bless you with Love and Abundance!

It would be lovely to hear your responses to ideas shared and how *Prosper Anyway* is blessing your life. You can send an email to me at:

carolynljennings@gmail.com

In *subject line* th ank you for writing: Prosper Anyway

34469280R00076

Made in the USA
San Bernardino, CA
29 May 2016